CHEF'S PSA

BAD SOUS
GOOD CHEF

A Journey of Mentorship and Growth

OTHER CHEF'S PSA BOOKS

How Not to Be the Biggest Idiot in the Kitchen

Culinary Leadership Fundamentals

The Line Cook Survival Manual

Kitchen Art of War

BAD SOUS GOOD CHEF

A Journey of Mentorship and Growth

ANDRÉ NATERA

Dedication

I dedicate this book not only to all the sous chefs out there but also to the chefs mentoring the next generation, including my own mentors, Patrick Mitchell and Kirk Bachmann. In my current work, I engage with chefs from various backgrounds, and a common complaint is the shortage of skilled cooks and chefs. The only way for this industry to move forward is by having the previous generation pass on their knowledge to the next.

This book is dedicated to the chefs who take the time to mentor, coach, and teach the upcoming generation of sous chefs and chefs. It is also dedicated to the sous chefs who have the courage to step into leadership roles, remaining open-minded and willing to learn. You are shaping the future of the industry, which is a significant responsibility. Embrace it with wisdom, passion, intelligence, strategy, and hard work.

Table of Contents

Preface

The idea for this book originated during my weekly Q&A sessions on Instagram. I've always harbored a passion for mentoring chefs and cooks, having been fortunate enough to benefit from exceptional mentors myself. It's my way of giving back. However, I recognized that numerous cooks and chefs don't have access to mentorship - a privilege I had perhaps taken for granted, and hadn't fully appreciated.

From day one, I had access to wise chefs who, for some reason, were always willing to share their wisdom with me. Maybe my relentless questioning about food inspired them, or perhaps they noticed my attentive nature whenever they spoke.

Through my involvement with Chef's PSA, I've realized that many chefs harbor the same fears and queries about the industry, yet don't know who to approach. This inspired me to write a book addressing the many questions novices in the industry might have when they feel they have no one to confide in. It could be due to fear, or perhaps their mentors are simply not available.

I conceived the idea of structuring the book as a fictional conversation to answer as many questions as possible - questions

I've been asked or have asked myself. Much of the dialogue in this book is based on things I've conveyed to those I mentor, or advice my mentors imparted to me. Not all the advice will be suitable for every chef, so feel free to pick what resonates with your style. The intention behind this book is for it to be applicable not only to your actions in the kitchen but, if I've done my job well, to life as a whole.

Introduction

Introduction

Becoming a Sous Chef: A Pivotal Role

When you first start out fresh from culinary school, sous chefs can seem like the cool kids from high school. In terms of culinary athleticism, they're the varsity team, and a good sous chef is like a star quarterback. The sous chef position seems aspirational, distant. All the cooks in the kitchen aspire to be like them, copying their mannerisms, behaviors, and trying to emulate their cooking. Many cooks want to be adopted by the sous chef as their favorite. At times, the head chef seems so distant and far above, they're not relatable to the entry-level cook. But the sous chef is close, like an older sibling.

In most kitchen operations, there's typically one sous chef for every five cooks. If you aspire to be a head chef, you will most likely have to pass through the role of sous chef. Skipping this step is more the exception than the rule, and it's not recommended because you'll be missing critical learning points needed in your development.

Facing Challenges and Overcoming Insecurity

When the time finally comes for you to become the sous chef, you may be overqualified and confident. However, this is unlikely. In most scenarios, you'll be nervous, underprepared, and

4

possibly in over your head. This is a frightening scenario because it seems inevitable that failure is around the corner. Yet, every successful chef has been in your shoes and made it through. No matter what endeavor you undertake, you'll always start out inexperienced and perhaps a little clumsy. But don't let the fear of the unknown hold you back from progressing in your career. You're going to have to take the leap at some point if you ever want to be the head chef. Everyone was once a beginner—be brave.

A Personal Anecdote

When I was a sous chef, I was very insecure about myself and my skills. I wanted to be the best, but I was afraid to be around others who were better or who I thought might be. I was a sous chef at 21 years old and worked in one of the top Italian restaurants in the city. There was a cool new restaurant opening, and although I wanted to work there, I lacked the confidence to apply. I told my chef mentor, and he looked puzzled. He said, "You're good, not sure why you're afraid to work there?" In retrospect, the food at this other place was simple; it was just out of my comfort zone. But time and wisdom allow you to see things later. My chef saw this and sat me down, giving me a talk and a confidence boost. I am grateful to this day for his time and guidance.

The Journey from Bad Sous Chef to Good Sous Chef

In my culinary career, being a sous chef was one of my most enjoyable positions. I thoroughly enjoyed it because I felt like I had a little bit of power and was able to flex on my peers. Not only that, but I felt like I finally had credibility and was able to introduce items on the menu. It felt good teaching the younger cooks some new skills and techniques that they didn't know, and rest assured, I used my two years of additional experience on them as the upper hand to demonstrate my superiority. I laugh at this now—I knew nothing then.

One of the best things for me and my career as sous chef was that I had great chef mentors. Without them, I can't sit here and say that I'd be the chef that I am.

Chapter 1
The Promotion

The Promotion

Freshly promoted to a new sous chef position, Juno had been working under his head chef, Kris, since graduating from culinary school. Kris seemed like an old sage, a Yoda from Star Wars, from Juno's perspective. Juno saw Kris as not only a mentor but also a trusted friend who seemed to have all the answers. Despite Juno's best efforts, he was never able to stump the wise chef.

Kris always seemed to be at the restaurant working, the first one there and the last to leave. Kris was an old-timer, tough but kind, who understood that the future was with chefs like Juno.

Kris liked Juno, recognizing something in him that Kris had seen in his younger self. He saw Juno's true potential, something Juno did not see in themselves. Juno struggled with confidence, and Kris acknowledged this, occasionally pushing Juno right to the edge, where he might fail, only to pull back.

Juno had recently accepted a sous chef position at one of the city's top restaurants. Many of Juno's culinary school friends and fellow cooks worked at this restaurant. They reached out to Juno, asking him to join when the sous chef position opened up. Juno was a cook under Kris with no sous chef or leadership experience, but Kris had been mentoring and preparing Juno to become a great sous chef. Kris had been teaching not only the fundamentals of cooking but also the art of running a kitchen through organization, discipline, and strategic thinking. Kris was thrilled when Juno announced his acceptance of the new position.

On Juno's last day at the restaurant, his anxiety was sky-high; all he could think about was starting the new job as a sous chef. These were close friends, and now Juno would be their boss - they'd all come up together. How could Juno possibly instruct them? Juno knew their good and bad habits. What if Juno had to discipline them or even fire one of them? What if they were better cooks than him? What if Juno wasn't ready to be a sous chef?

As these thoughts flooded Juno's mind, the idea of not leaving at all had also crossed. Continue working under Chef Kris; Juno was afraid to leave the nest. With a rush of feelings and anxiety, and before closing time, Juno sought out one last conversation with Kris. Finding him in the back office, drinking coffee and playing chess alone, Juno asked to sit down. "What's troubling you?" Kris asked. Juno responded, "I'm afraid. I don't want to go to the new job. I'm not ready. I have a lot to learn still. I don't think I'm good enough."

"I think my friends are better than me, and I'm going to have a hard time telling them what to do. I've never had to be harsh to anyone in my life. I still have so much to learn about cooking, and how can I teach people when I don't know certain things?" Kris replied, "Sit down, grab a cup of coffee, and let's play a game of chess. We can talk."

9

As Juno sat down and looked at Kris's stern face and piercing eyes, time seemed to stop. The clock on the wall was not moving, and the restaurant went silent and empty. Kris looked over at Juno and said, "What are you afraid of?" Juno answered, "I'm afraid I'll be a bad sous chef."

Kris leaned back in the chair, considering Juno's words before speaking. "Juno, fear is natural, especially when you're about to take on new responsibilities. It's a sign that you care about doing a good job. But you can't let fear control you or hold you back. You've worked hard, and you've learned a lot from me and from your own experiences. It's time for you to apply that knowledge and grow as a chef."

"I have so many questions. I'm not sure where to begin," Juno said, his eyes fixated on the chessboard between them, uncertain of the next move. The dimly lit restaurant around them seemed to hold its breath as they continued their conversation over steaming cups of coffee.

Juno: Chef, I need your guidance.
Kris: Well, let's start at the beginning. What are you most afraid of with this new job?

Juno: If I'm being honest, I'm afraid I'm not good enough, and I don't know if I'm ready.
Kris: The fact of the matter is, you'll never be ready if you don't try. There's only one way to truly know, and that's to dive into the deep end. Is anyone ever truly ready? You don't know what you don't know. But that shouldn't stop you from moving forward. You're paralyzed with fear, but the truth of the matter is, it's all in your mind. Your body is capable; you're trained, you

10

know how to cook, you've watched me lead this brigade. You know the right thing to do. The question is, are you willing to do it?

Juno paused, taking a sip of coffee and absorbing Kris's words. Glancing around the empty restaurant, recalling the countless hours spent learning and growing in this very space.

Juno: Were you afraid when you got your first sous chef job?
Kris: Of course, I was afraid; it's natural. And realistically, I was probably in over my head and definitely not qualified. But it didn't stop me from seizing the opportunity. I could sit back and constantly say I'm not ready, and I will be ready when this happens or when that happens. But the only way to truly get experience is to do the job. Everyone is a beginner at some point; you must get off zero.

Juno: But I don't know everything about cooking. How am I supposed to teach people when I don't know? Do I fake it? Do I lie?
Kris: There's no point in faking it or lying; people will see through it. You might think you're fooling others, but trust me, you're not. Cooks and chefs who have been in the kitchen for a long time can recognize weakness, and lying and faking it is a form of weakness.

Not knowing is not weak because we all begin in the state of not knowing. It's from not knowing that we begin to learn. Every great chef is a perpetual student; the more they learn, the more they realize they don't know. When you begin your career as a cook, everything seems complicated. Then when you get a little bit of experience, you think you know everything.

Once you really start to master the arts, you realize you know nothing. And when you finally become a master, you realize it was easy the whole time. However, you cannot arrive at the state of realizing that it is easy before you realize that you know nothing, and you never will.

Juno's gaze returned to the chessboard, his hand hovering above a piece and considering the next move.

Juno: So, what do I do when I don't know something?
Kris: What any person does when they don't know something and are unafraid of what others think of them: let them know you don't know and ask how to do it. There's nothing wrong with not knowing, asking, and learning. There's something wrong when you pretend that you know, and you do not, and you ruin it, wasting time and resources, and end up looking foolish.

Being nervous and afraid about not knowing will prevent you from knowing. Seek difficulty in the kitchen and learn the things that you don't know. Seek to understand techniques and methods with which you are unfamiliar and learn them. This is the journey of a chef: to seek out things they don't know, acquire knowledge, and then express it on a plate.

Juno: What if they talk badly about me behind my back that I don't know something?
Kris: They will talk about you behind your back. Is this going to stop you from doing your job and improving? You realize they're going to talk about you behind your back if you are good or if you are bad, when you know and when you don't know. When you succeed and when you don't. This is human nature and does not make you special or the center of attention.

If they weren't talking about you, you might want to question why not?

Juno: So, you're saying it's OK for them to talk bad about me behind my back?

Kris: I'm not saying it's OK, I'm saying it's going to happen, but this is something that has happened to every single chef that has come before you, and you, my young apprentice, are no exception to this rule. You are going to be in a position of leadership and you are going to sometimes do things that are unpopular. You are going to be held to a standard that others don't hold themselves to but will judge you harshly. But this is no reason to be afraid or to worry or lose sleep. Because what they think of you should not affect you one bit.

Juno: Do you think people complain about you?

Kris: I know they complain about me. It's to be expected. I would honestly be surprised if they didn't. When you assume a leadership role, you also take on the good and bad that comes with it. It is human nature for people to complain about their boss, even when they respect them. It's similar to a child who might get upset with their parents and vent to a sibling. This doesn't mean that they don't love their parents.

Juno: When you find out someone is complaining about you, do you feel differently about them?

Kris: No, not one bit. If you and your siblings were complaining about your parents and someone who was a non-family member joined the conversation and started to speak badly about them, you would most likely defend your parents. It's the old expression, "I'm allowed to talk bad about my parents, but you are not." The same holds true for a chef and their cooks.

13

The chef understands that the cooks will speak badly about them behind their back when they need to blow off some steam but hopes that they will defend them when an outsider tries to join in.

Juno: What happens when someone comes and tells you that others on your team were speaking badly about you?
Kris: I trust them less than those who were speaking badly. They have broken the trust and the right of the team to blow off steam in confidence. And in doing so, they've tried to gain some sort of favoritism from me. I would ask them why they didn't defend me in the moment, instead of trying to make me feel a certain way about the other cooks.

Juno: What if they were speaking badly about you and planning against you?
Kris: Then this is where your wisdom and discretion comes in. Many times, you're surrounded by snakes. Not all of them are dangerous. Some are venomous snakes, such as vipers and cobras, and others are harmless garden snakes. You must be wise to recognize that and know how to handle them appropriately.

Juno: What if my team sees me fail?
Kris: Then they know you're human. Everyone fails, but how you handle the failure is what will determine what happens next. You could use it as an excuse not to try again and become stagnant, or you can use it as an opportunity to learn and get better.

Juno: What would you, as my mentor, think of me if you saw me fail?
Kris: If you were learning from your failures, I would encourage you to fail some more. Because it is in failure where you have the most amount of learning. Greatness and knowledge are forged in

14

failure. It's the difficulty that defines you. The greater the difficulty, the greater the person, especially when overcoming that difficulty. However, if you were not learning from your failures, then I would advise you to step back and analyze why you keep repeating the same mistakes. Making the same mistakes repeatedly after a certain point becomes a choice.

Juno: Isn't it a chef's job to get mad at someone when they fail?
Kris: It's a chef's job to deliver exceptional food, ensure smooth service, and create a positive culture that allows people to grow and flourish. Getting mad is an individual's emotion tied to a specific person and how they react. It is not tied to a position, title, or responsibility.

Juno: Even after all that, I'm still not sure if I have a clear direction on what to do when I'm afraid of failing.
Kris: What is your goal?

Juno: I want to be a great chef!
Kris: Then remember, on the other side of fear lies greatness. Remind yourself of this every time you are afraid to start something. It has never failed me, and I promise it won't ever fail you.

Chapter 2
Building Trust

Building Trust

Juno's mind was spinning, reflecting on everything that had been discussed. He was still not fully confident and had many more questions for Kris. "Checkmate," said Kris. "I'm sorry," Juno replied. "Checkmate," Kris repeated, "You're not paying attention; this was a rather easy game." Juno had been so engrossed in the conversation that he forgot about playing chess. Kris, on the other hand, was fully immersed in both the conversation and the game.

Both sipped their coffee as Kris sat back in the chair, eyeing Juno thoughtfully. "Do you have any more questions? I feel like you're still thinking," said Kris. Juno responded, "Yes, I still have a lot of questions. You answered most of my general fear-related questions, but how do I maintain relationships with my friends? These are people I went to culinary school with, and I'm worried." Kris reset the chessboard and suggested, "Let's play another game and continue this conversation." Juno played as white and opened with pawn to E4.

Juno: What is the best way to work with people who are your friends?
Kris: When you're in a position of leadership, it doesn't matter if they're your friends or people you might not like. You must treat

everyone with dignity and respect and maintain professionalism at work. How you feel about them personally shouldn't affect how you feel about them professionally. I've worked with many people that I liked personally but professionally might not be the best fit.

Take my brother, the carpenter, for example. As much as I love my brother, I would not want him to be my sous chef. Yet, if I found someone extremely capable and a good fit for the job, even if I didn't like them the most outside of work, if they are professional and respectful inside of work, I would hire them over my brother.

Juno: But that still doesn't answer the question. Because I do have friendships with these people, we go and hang out together after work. I've known them for years; I think of them as my brothers and sisters.

Kris: People respect boundaries. It gives parameters so people know what they can and cannot do. When lines are crossed, there need to be consequences for the actions. However, if they cross the line and there are no consequences, then the boundaries are imaginary and pointless. It's important that you speak to your friends and let them know from the beginning that you take your job seriously and that you need to establish professional boundaries with them while at work.

Juno: How do I balance my friendship with them and still have them respect me?

Kris: As strange as this may sound, they will respect you more if you maintain professionalism at work. You will demonstrate strength and character, and people respect that. You are doing them no favors if you are letting them get away with things and

17

showing favoritism. You are hurting them in the long run, and if you are truly their friend, you would want the best for them. Additionally, if you show favoritism to them, you will lose the respect of those people who are not in your circle of friends. This will lead to more challenges in the kitchen. And rest assured, no one is fooled, including your new chef.

Juno: What if they get upset with me because I'm not one of them anymore and I'm not letting them get away with certain things?

Kris: Friends uplift each other and want success for you and for them. You letting them get away with things is not doing them any favors; you are not helping them, you're not lifting them up. Them speaking badly about you is not lifting you up. What type of friends do you have? I promise you that if you're not making your friends better and they are not making you better, then you might be in a relationship where you're making each other worse.

Juno: Do you think my friends will turn against me?

Kris: It's difficult to say, as I'm unsure how you're going to approach this situation and establish boundaries. However, what I will say is that most likely, at first, you will be celebrated. Your friends will be happy that one of their own has made it. Your victory will be their victory. Most people's natural inclination is to see how they will benefit from this situation. If they see that there's no benefit because you have established boundaries and kept the relationship professional, this will cause dissension. People will say you've changed, and the position has gotten to your head. You have now become one of the others and no longer remember what it was like to be a cook. Of course, this is not the case, but these are the growing pains of leadership.

Juno: How do I handle a situation of conflict when one of my friends is involved?

Kris: Always handle every situation with dignity and respect, listen more than you speak, and seek to understand. Be fair in your decisions and let friendships not interfere with good judgment. It's wise to tell your friends where you stand and let them know to never put you in a situation where you will have to hold them accountable because, indeed, you will hold them accountable.

Juno: What if I have to fire someone?

Kris: The same principle holds true: be respectful. The person has given you their time and energy working in your kitchen. They've likely built bonds with others that worked there, including yourself. This is an uncomfortable situation for everybody, not just you; it's more uncomfortable for them. Be respectful, straightforward, and let them walk out with their head held high. Keep the matter confidential out of respect for the individual. Sharing someone else's dirty laundry lets everyone else on the team know that you will also do the same to them if the situation were theirs.

Juno: How can I support my friends in the kitchen with their own growth and development?

Kris: These are the questions you need to be asking! Your job as a leader is to help others grow and develop. Not just for your friends but for everyone that works with you. However, since we are speaking of your friends and you have personal relationships with them, this will allow you to speak more candidly with them. Be the type of chef that you would like to work for. The most important job you have as a leader is developing others, if you're not doing that then you must question what you're doing at all.

That is managing not leading.

Juno: What if people say I'm showing favoritism by helping my friends?

Kris: It's only natural that you will show favoritism you're human after all. But you need to be aware of this and catch yourself when you find yourself doing this and correct it. As I said earlier you should be developing everyone on your team. If your team knows you care about all of them there is no favoritism. Everyone needs to have a purpose and a sense of belonging on your team. It's your job as the leader to ensure that everyone feels welcome. But also know that not everyone wants to be helped. People must be willing to help themselves first. You don't want to swim for them, you want them to learn how to swim.

Juno: I know you're my mentor and you've spent a lot of time developing me, but would you fire me?

Kris: I give you the energy you put out in return like holding up a mirror. It would never be me who fired you, it would be you, who fired yourself. I've created boundaries and you understand the consequences of your actions should you cross them.

Chapter 3
Holding Others Accountable

Holding Others Accountable

They sat there, both silent for a moment; a lot had been discussed, a lot had been said. Juno playing chess with Kris, seems like a game only one person was playing. Again checkmate, and again checkmate over and over again. They've played this game many times over the years and the result was always the same.

Even though the night was late, the coffee was starting to kick in and the caffeine rush of energy, mixed with anxiety about the new job, made Juno break the silence.

Juno: When you become a chef, is it important to hold people accountable?
Kris: Only one thing is more important than that.
Juno: What is that?
Kris: Holding yourself accountable. When you're in a position of leadership and you have accountability and authority over others it means more if you're able to hold yourself accountable also. Do as I say not as I do is a fast route to losing the respect of the team. If you cannot hold yourself accountable, holding others accountable is an exercise in vanity.

Juno looked puzzled not sure if he was following this

conversation. Time was still stopped, how long had this conversation been going on? Had it been hours? It felt like days had passed.

Juno: How do I hold myself accountable?
Kris: Only preach what you practice, don't act as if you are above the law. Be willing to do what you ask others to do. And when you ask others to do it, ensure that you're not asking them because you feel you are above that work. When you find yourself slipping correct it, admit your error and if needed apologize.

Juno: How can I ensure I'm being fair?
Kris: Always measure performance, set expectations, and hold everyone accountable to the same standards, regardless of your relationship with them. In the kitchen, the only measure of a chef is their ability to create consistently good food. It's the social currency of a cook. It doesn't matter whether you like them or not, whether they are tall or short, purple or pink. Focus on the performance and product.

Juno: How do I hold them accountable?
Kris: As a chef, sometimes you need to lift your head up off the board and look around. Correcting someone doesn't mean belittling or humiliating them; it means addressing the behavior and showing them the right way to do things. When demonstrating, you must also explain why something is done a certain way. Failing to include the 'why' leaves room for interpretation, and in most cases, their interpretation won't be in your favor.

Juno: What if they don't listen to me?

23

Kris: If this is the first time it's happening, it's important to address it immediately. People tend to push boundaries with new leaders, and over time, the drift can cause the kitchen to no longer resemble its original intent. The team will test you, especially if you are their friend or a new leader. It's your responsibility to push back respectfully but let them know you won't be walked over. If you allow them to walk over you, they'll continue to do so. People will give you the same energy back; if you treat others with respect, they will respect you in return. You must also carry yourself with respect; if they sense weakness in you, they'll become like sharks smelling blood in the water.

Juno: What if I find myself in a situation where I'm in over my head?

Kris: Rest assured; those situations will come. You won't have the answer for everything when you're new in your position. If your chef is available for guidance, ask them. If they are unavailable, consider what you think they would do in this situation. And if you're still unsure, do what you believe is right.

Juno: What is the best way to ensure I demonstrate empathy while holding people accountable?

Kris: Understand where people are coming from, why mistakes are being made, and put yourself in their shoes. Remember what it was like to be in their position when you first started and how you felt when people spoke to you in certain ways. Remember, be the type of chef that you would like to work for. This is one of the most important rules.

Chapter 4
Leading a Team

Leading a Team

Every clock on the wall was still. The restaurant fell silent. As the two chefs sat there, Juno began to think about all the time they had spent working together. He had started out knowing nothing and was now getting ready to take on his first sous chef role. What Juno admired most was the leadership style Kris exhibited. This is the type of leader Juno hoped to become one day. Kris had a remarkable memory and seemed never to forget anything. Chef always had the right answers at the right times, even for the most ridiculous questions. Juno had tried many times to stump Kris but never succeeded. Chef Kris was never sleeping on the job, and the job was 24 hours.

Juno: How do you know everything? Why do you always seem to have an answer? How is it that you never forget?
Kris: Do you remember your home address? Do you remember your birthday? Do you remember when you graduated from culinary school?
Juno: Of course, I do.
Kris: Why is it that you remember all that?
Juno: Because obviously, those things are important to me.
Kris: Well, everything is important to me; that's why I remember everything. And in the kitchen, you must be mindful that everything is important.

26

Juno: What do you mean everything is important?

Kris: I mean what I said, EVERYTHING is important. From the way you walk in the door, to how you set your station, to the ingredients you choose to use, to the cloth you use to wipe the plate. Every decision you make, every action you take is important to the end product.

Juno: So, are you saying as a leader I need to be mindful of every decision I make? That seems impossible.

Kris: That is exactly what I am saying. You should be able to explain the reasoning behind any action you take to anyone who asks. Is this an arbitrary decision that you've made without any thought? That's careless and shows you are on autopilot and not thinking for yourself.

Every action you make needs to be deliberate and thoughtful. If you want to achieve excellent results, you need to have excellent actions. You cannot begin with bad ingredients and end up with a good dish. Similarly, you cannot begin with bad actions and end up with good results. Your limited scope of thinking leads you to believe this is impossible, however, every great chef out there is only great because they did what others thought was impossible.

Juno: So, when you're leading a team, you have to consider everything?

Kris: Yes, precisely! Everything is important. Excellence is in the details; it's thinking about the things that other people don't, that separates you.

In this game of chess that we're playing, you only play the moves you know. I play all the moves you know and all the moves I know. Then I consider all the moves I don't know. This is why I

27

win, and you remain perplexed

Juno began thinking about the constant checkmate that he was in. And started to consider he needed to think more strategically as Kris had instructed. Juno began to think about the team and leading them. Some of them were friends from school and used to think they were better chefs. Now Juno has the upper hand and couldn't wait to demonstrate that to them.

Juno: There are some parts that excite me about taking this new job. One in particular is that now I will be able to show my fellow chefs who's in charge.
Kris: How do you plan on showing them who's in charge?

Juno: I will be the sous chef. This position means I am superior. If they were superior, then they would be the sous chef. It's as simple as that.
Kris: Exactly how are you superior?

Juno: I'm the sous chef speaks for itself, the same reason you are the head chef that makes you superior to everyone else that works here.
Kris: What you fail to realize is I'm not superior to anyone that works here, I work for them as much as they work for me. I am nothing without the team I cannot cook all this food by myself, and I cannot serve all the dinner guests. I cannot wash all the dishes. In this game, I am simply a piece on the chess board, but all pieces have their value. Never forget that a pawn can checkmate a king. The title is just that, a title. You still must earn it daily through your actions and leadership.

Juno: So, what's the point of being a sous chef if you're not

28

superior?

Kris: As the expression goes, all rivers flow into the ocean because it is lower than them. You must humble yourself and others will follow. Acting superior is just that, an act. It is the job of a leader to work for the people they are leading. Inspire them and respect them, they are your team and are vital to your daily success. Each one of them is important so treat them as such. If you treat them as if they are not important then why will they stay? You can rest assured at the moment they have an opportunity to turn on you they will.

Juno: What causes someone to turn on me?

Kris: Humiliating them, embarrassing them, treating them as if they are not part of the team, acting as the exception to the rule, and not respecting them as an individual.

Juno: How can I tell them what to do then?

Kris: Let's use the word ask instead. But even if we weren't going to argue over the semantics of the words used. Letting people know what their job is can be done in one or two ways. It could be done respectfully, or it could be done with poisonous words. Poisonous words will eventually be turned on you, however, respect will be given back to you. I shouldn't have to point out the obvious better choice here.

Juno: Then, as a leader, how can I inspire my team and ensure they remain loyal?

Kris: While there is not a single answer, I can tell you that one way to build loyalty among your team is to be loyal to them as well. Show that you have a genuine interest in their betterment, invest in them, teach them, mentor them, and when you see them drifting away, bring them back.

29

Juno: Is it that easy?

Kris: Certainly not. You must work on creating a culture where people can thrive. A culture of respect and discipline is the foundation for a successful kitchen.

Juno: Discipline?

Kris: Yes, discipline. We could take this to mean two different things. The first is the discipline to do difficult things consistently, even when you don't want to do them. It's the discipline to ensure that the knife cuts are always perfect, the towels are always neatly stacked and folded, and at the end of the night, everything is cleaned meticulously. This form of discipline requires everyone to be on board. If anyone is not on board, it will create resentment among team members who feel they are carrying out most of the work while others get off easy.

Juno: What is the other form of discipline that you're talking about then?

Kris: The other form of discipline a leader needs to have is more along the line of consequences. Every action must have consequences, negative or positive, and you want to ensure that no one is exempt. If the standard is that everyone must clean together and leave together, then there must be consequences for the person who decides not to be a part of that. This will maintain order in your kitchen.

Juno: Is that all I need to do to have a successful kitchen?

Kris: No, every kitchen team needs a mission, vision, and purpose. Every individual on your team needs to know what the mission is, which could be, becoming the best restaurant in a particular market. The vision is where we are going together; this is the inspiration that tells me why I want to be on this team.

30

The purpose is every individual's unique role on the team. They understand how they affect the outcome and have a certain sense of responsibility. If someone cannot answer what your mission, vision, and purpose is, then they may begin to look for other places to work.

With a furrowed brow Juno contemplated the difficulty in the new role. Beginning to wonder if they were ready to leave.

Juno: This is something I've wanted ever since I began cooking. I've always wanted to be the chef in charge.

Kris: The position looks glamorous, and everyone thinks the job is easy and fun. But once you're in the position, you realize it's much more difficult than you expected. Everyone wants the title, but not everyone really wants the job. The title is nice to brag about, but that wears off quickly when the real job difficulty sets in.

Juno: What is one of the more difficult parts of the job of being a leader?

Kris: There's not just one difficulty, as there are multiple challenges. One is the burden of leadership. You build relationships with others and begin to care for the people you work with. But there will be times when you must hold them accountable or even let them go. People may not see the distinction between you and the job. Making tough decisions and delivering tough messages is the burden of the leader.

Juno: What do I do when I don't agree with the decision that I have to deliver?

Kris: In many cases, you may not understand why you must deliver certain decisions to the team. But this is the role you

31

accepted. Unless you are willing to return the money that you are getting paid to be in a leadership role, then you must assume the responsibility. You cannot have both. However, if you must deliver a decision that is unethical, illegal, or immoral, then it's best to keep your integrity versus your job.

Juno: What is another difficulty I may face?
Kris: Another difficulty is the burden of responsibility when things aren't going well. Your first instinct will be to blame others, but when you assume the role of leader, you also assume responsibility for others' actions. If you have the authority to tell them what to do, then you have the responsibility when they don't do what they're supposed to.

Juno: As much as I don't like hearing this, what is another difficulty of leadership that I may face?
Kris: Another difficulty is surrounding yourself with people who won't be honest with you. People will be dishonest with you when you're in a position of leadership, not to benefit you but usually to benefit themselves. Your jokes will be a little funnier, your wit will be sharper, your food will taste better, and everyone will likely agree with your decisions even when they don't.

Juno: The position of leader sounds difficult. I can see why many people don't want to assume the position.
Kris: The person who learns how to cook will always have a job, and the person who learns how to lead will usually be their boss. Being an excellent cook is the gatekeeper, but as you ascend the ladder, you will learn that you need skills greater than cooking. With leadership, you could go far.

Juno: Is it important for me as a leader to rescue them from failure?

Kris: Failure and difficulty are your greatest teachers. It is important that people fail and face difficulty; this is how they will learn and become better. However, if their failure impacts the guest or the rest of the team, then you, as the leader, need to know when to step in.

Juno: So how do I become a great leader?

Kris: Discipline yourself first, treat others with respect, create an environment where others can learn and prosper, and ensure everyone on your team has a purpose. Celebrate the wins together; this is the success of a team. Accept responsibility when things aren't great; this is the responsibility of the leader. Help your team learn to stand on their own two feet.

Juno: Thank you for all the advice. It seems like I have a lot to learn and grow in this new role.

Kris: You're welcome, Juno. Remember, leadership is a journey, and you will continue to learn and evolve as you go. Keep an open mind, be willing to listen, and always strive to improve yourself and your team. That's what makes a great leader and chef.

Chapter 5
Managing a Kitchen

Managing a Kitchen

Juno's mind was becoming more at ease, as many of the
leadership questions were being answered. Juno knew that Kris's
advice was valuable, but it was Juno's responsibility to put it into
action. Thinking about the daily operation in the kitchen and
what some strategies might be. Juno wanted to be a great chef
and run a great kitchen. Kris ran a well-oiled machine with the
restaurant and Juno wanted to understand how to translate that
knowledge to the new place.

Juno: Can we talk about how to run the day-to-day operations in
a kitchen?
Kris: Of course, you might even say that's my specialty.
Juno: "I thought your specialty was chicken Alfredo?" Juno said,
laughing.

Juno: I have a lot of questions that are specific to being a good
chef. Where should I spend the most amount of my time?
Kris: Every single kitchen is different, and it's important that you
assess the situation. As I said earlier, lift your eyes up from the
cutting board and look around. Your responsibility as the sous
chef is to ensure smooth service. To ensure that, you need to
make sure that everyone has the tools they need to do their job.
The product must be fresh, and the recipes must be followed.

In every moment, you need to be aware of the situation.

Juno: What's the best way to ensure people have fresh products on the line?

Kris: First, you need to expect them to have fresh product. Make sure they understand what the standard is. Many cooks don't know the difference between good, fresh products and bad, incorrectly prepared, or spoiled products. They don't have a frame of reference. Next, you need to make sure you are walking the line and the production area daily. Inspect the mise en place visually and taste it as well. It's much easier to look at something that is raw product like vegetables, fruits, and at times, meats, and tell if they are fresh. However, with prepared items like sauces and soups, you need to taste them because visuals will not give you the whole story.

Juno: Does that mean I only need to taste a few things?

Kris: No, a chef's palate is their superpower. Taste everything, season it and adjust, then taste it again, make any adjustments, and taste once more. Taste things when they are good and taste things when they are bad. You will start to build a flavor memory profile in your mind. This will help you build flavors as well as correct them. But while tasting, pay attention to other things like color, for example, and smell. If you've tasted something 1,000 times and you notice the smell is off or the color is, you will know that it's not correct. You will be able to know that the recipe wasn't followed accurately. Eventually, you will be able to smell things and know that they need seasoning.

Juno: Great, this is what I want to know. What is your strategy when you're tasting and inspecting the line?

Kris: When I inspect the line, I assume I have already inspected the produce upon arrival, and I know what was fresh. So, when I walk down the line, I look at the cut produce and am inspecting the accuracy of the work and the freshness of the ingredient. As I mentioned, I can do this visually. As I walk down the saucier line, I smell the stocks and sauces and then taste them as well. I adjust as needed, and then I look for finished ingredients on the line such as purees, vinaigrettes, and other accoutrements. I taste these to ensure they are seasoned correctly and fresh. I also inspect them visually to make sure they are appealing and made correctly.

Juno: What do you do when you find something that is made incorrectly? How do you correct the cooks?
Kris: I first ask them if they've tasted it; that's where we begin. Let's assume they have not; then I will walk them through the process of tasting it with me and explain to them what they're tasting. I break down every nuance of flavor. This will help them develop their palate, acting as a force multiplier for your culinary operation. If they have tasted it and didn't notice anything was wrong with it, I will also coach them on how to notice subtle flavors. The unacceptable answer is if they have tasted it, know it is incorrect, and still decided to serve it. This is an act of carelessness and does not represent someone I would want on my team.

Juno: I'd like to talk about how you organize the production. How do you know what to do first?
Kris: There are multiple right answers here, and every chef can explain to you a different method in which they prefer. However, let's assume you need a simple order of hierarchy for your prep list.

If you have a dish, for example, that dish has steak, potatoes, carrots, sauce, and garnish. The most important item on the dish is the steak; without it, the dish cannot be sold. You cannot explain to the customer that the steak dish they want isn't available, but they could have the potatoes, carrots, sauce, and garnish. More than likely, the dish will become unavailable for the evening. However, every other ingredient in that dish can be substituted except for the steak. So, which one should you ensure that you have first?

Juno: Clearly the steak.
Kris: Excellent, and of those needed to make the dish exceptional and satisfying for the guest, which one bears the least importance?

Juno: Probably the garnish, assuming it's maybe some chopped herbs.
Kris: I agree with you on this, so that would mean it is the least important on the prep list. So, to organize your prep list, the most important thing being the steak in this case needs to be completed first, and the least important thing being the garnish needs to be the last thing on the prep list. The remaining items need to be sorted by order of importance and prep time. If something takes longer to prep and is more difficult but important, then it needs to rank higher on your prep list. If something is easy to prep and less important for the dish, then it can rank lower.

Juno: But what about stocks, ferments, or braises that need to be made well in advance?
Kris: I've given you a simple idea, and you have found a way to overcomplicate it. There are always going to be exceptions to the

rule. And if you ask me a question, it would be impossible for me to answer every single variable that may arise with an answer that fits all.

When you have items that require longer preparation, then you must think further ahead, and most likely, this would not be on your daily prep list for that day's service. This would be on a prep list that is for future service. So, as I said, when organizing your prep list, if something requires longer than a day to prepare, then clearly you were going to be unable to serve the dish that day anyway.

Juno: So, should there be prep lists also for things that are further out?

Kris: Yes, precisely. If something needs to be preserved, fermented, a stock that needs to be made, or a braise, you need to factor in the time it takes to make that in advance of when you need it for service. If you have chickens that need to be brined and the brine takes 24 hours before they can be served, then you need to factor that into your prep list; you need to be working ahead.

Juno: Does this prep list apply to catering as well?

Kris: This is a yes, no, maybe answer. It's going to depend on what is being served, and how long it will take you to prepare it. In many catering operations, frozen products must be thawed out, which requires you to pull them two to three days prior to an event. Sometimes meats and vegetables are prepared the day before. Other places prefer to prepare the day of. But one thing is certain: you should always be prepared in advance.

Juno: Should prep lists be written out? Or does everyone just know what they're doing?

Kris: Depending on the size, scale, and complexity, you might not need a prep list. However, even the best chefs use prep lists. Why risk forgetting? A poor pen still outperforms a sharp memory, so always jot things down.

Juno: What about food deliveries and ordering? What are some things to look out for?

Kris: There's a lot to look out for; this isn't such a simple question. However, I can tell you that quality and price should be the two guiding factors in every decision. As a chef, your pursuit should constantly be towards superior quality ingredients. Access to better ingredients inevitably results in tastier food. With regards to price, when you're in a position of leadership, you are also in a position of financial stewardship. It's important to get the best quality product for the best price available. That is being a responsible chef.

Juno: How do I make sure my vendors don't take advantage of me?

Kris: It's important that you keep them honest, check the pricing on invoices, weigh the product as it arrives, and when inferior products come to your door, send it back and request a refund immediately. The moment that you allow them to sneak in poor-quality products, you will be marked as an easy target. However, if they know that you catch everything, they will know not to mess around.

Juno: How do I handle the rush of service in a busy place?

Kris: Presuming you're in charge, maintaining your composure, and asserting control are essential. The rest of the culinary team is

40

watching you and feeds off your energy. If you're running around like a chicken with its head cut off, they will also do the same. If you're angry and volatile, you will make them nervous, and they will make mistakes. If you are calm and focused, they will also remain calm and focused. If they are not, your sense of calm can recalibrate them to a calm state.

Juno: What about calling the pass? What are some basic rules?
Kris: Some basic rules that apply to every kitchen are when you are calling, everyone should remain silent. The voice of the chef is the most important and needs to be listened to. People should not be coming into the kitchen, making noise when you are calling. It can be a distraction, and it is important that people understand when you are in the flow of service, everyone needs to remain 'awake and ready'.

After orders have been called, it is important that the cooks respond with acknowledgment. 'Yes, chef,' 'oui, chef,' or 'heard' are all different acknowledgments you may hear in a kitchen. The important point is that there is a response, signaling the person is present and focused on their task. It is important as the chef organizing the orders that you are the brains to the body which is the kitchen. You should be reminding the cooks of timing, keeping them in a good flow, controlling the service team in and out of the kitchen, and acting as the air traffic controller landing planes.

Juno: And with regards to techniques and trends, how do I stay sharp?
Kris: First, humble yourself enough to learn from everyone around you, whether you are their boss or they are yours, whether you like them or not. Don't dismiss the wisdom with the

41

wise; you can learn from everyone around you.

Second, immerse yourself in books and read the stories of chefs and the food they cooked, understand the history of food, learn about seasons and growing regions. Then use all the modern resources available to you to learn, whether it be online, social, or continuing education courses. Make yourself a perennial student. But most importantly, the best way to become a good cook, is to cook.

Chapter 6
Insights into the Culinary World

Insights Into the Culinary World

All of these discussions were planting seeds of understanding in Juno's mind. It was all starting to come together and make sense. Juno began to comprehend that learning is a process, and although it's impossible to know everything, Kris would always be there to provide guidance. Kris poured another cup of coffee, stirring in spoonfuls of sugar and a little bit of cream. After resetting the chessboard following a checkmate, there was still time for a few more games and, with those games, more lessons.

Ultimately, for a chef, the passion for creating food is the primary driver behind their decision to enter the field. And even though they had discussed a wide range of topics, Juno yearned to understand food better.

Juno: Can we talk about food and cooking?
Kris: I thought you'd never ask. All this talk about becoming a chef, leadership, and mentoring, yet we're overlooking a very important point, and that is cooking. When you're moving up into the sous chef role and beyond, understand that none of these opportunities will present themselves to you if you don't

first understand how to cook. If this was only an accounting or human resources job, then you wouldn't need chefs; you would hire accountants and human resources trainees to become managers and sous chefs. It is the technical proficiency that first gets you noticed to move up in the kitchen; it is the gatekeeper. Being a good cook comes first.

Juno: I thought when you become a sous chef, it's all about paperwork, meetings, and telling people what to do?
Kris: It can be; that's part of the job. But more important is being able to cook and create good food and amazing experiences for guests. There's not a restaurant owner out there that would prefer a good admin over a good cook when it comes to hiring a chef, at least not a wise one. That is not to say that administrative duties are not important, as they are. Understanding the business is what keeps it going. Creating great food is what keeps you going and keeps the customers coming back.

Juno: Let's start here, then. How can I understand food better?
Kris: Plant a garden, connect with it, and understand how it grows, when it grows, and why it grows. Understand when food is perfectly ripe or unripe. Understand that some of those seasons are very short. Understand how the color transforms the fruit and its flavor. Understand the perfect time to pick something for maximum flavor. Understand how things growing in proximity affect each other and add flavor to each other, not just from the point of the soil but also on the plate. When you put time, effort, and love into a garden, you will understand food from a greater perspective.

Juno: How can I develop my palate as a chef?

45

Kris: To develop your palate, you need to taste everything. As I mentioned earlier, you should taste things when they're bad and also when they're good. When you correct something, you should taste it and understand why it tastes different. When you're making a stock, you should taste it at the beginning, in the middle, and at the end. You should blindfold yourself or close your eyes and taste food, trying to figure out what it is you're tasting. You should taste a dish's components individually and then combined, and understand how they balance together. You should taste your food and the food of others. Understanding how to develop flavors and layer them is something that will take years for you to develop.

Juno: Do you think it's important to cook seasonally?
Kris: Yes, cooking seasonally allows you to serve ingredients when they are at their peak. In today's world, we are accustomed to getting anything year-round; we begin to lose our connection with nature. A new cook might not know that tomatoes don't grow in the winter. Research the traditions of cooking and understand why preserving, canning, fermenting, and having a root cellar were important. You can learn a lot about food when you understand the history of why things were done. If you wanted tomatoes in the winter, you might need to explore another option, and by exploring another option, you may develop a new flavor. Cooking seasonally is not limiting; if anything, it will challenge your creativity.

Juno: And cooking with local ingredients, is this also important?
Kris: Also very important. Learning what grows around you allows you to tell the story of the time and place. Connecting with the flora and fauna of your local environment, similar to planting a garden, will further expand your culinary knowledge.

46

Understanding the relationship between farmer, forager, artisan, and chef is not only important for the food but also for supporting your local community, who will, in turn, support you. Making relationships with locals who are producing great food will enhance your final product on the plate.

Juno: How do I tell a story through food?

Kris: You can create dishes for the sake of creating dishes, and if there is no emotional connection, they will taste good but lack soul. When you create a dish that has an emotional connection and you are able to tell a story, you can bridge the gap between chef and diner. All senses need to be stimulated, as do emotions. When you are able to evoke emotion through your food, you can create a new connection with your dinner guest. Food will taste differently if there is a story behind it, not just for you but also for the person trying it. You can take a bland dish and make it incredible with the right story.

Juno: How do I combine flavors?

Kris: When you understand how things grow, seasonality, locality, and have a story, you will understand how to combine flavors better. You will have developed your palate, and you will have a memory databank from which you can draw. If you only understood seasonality but not how things grow, you limit yourself. If you understood flavors but not locality, you would still be limited. When you combine them all, you can create exceptional flavor combinations. There are five tastes: sweet, sour, salty, bitter, and umami if you include it. Spicy, acrid, and pungent might introduce more complexity. With these few things, you can make an infinite amount of combinations. Your creativity will be limitless, but none of this works without proper culinary technique. You may have paint and paintbrushes, but

47

you are not a painter without your technique.

Juno: How do I learn and master different cooking techniques?
Kris: To learn and master different cooking techniques, you need to practice, experiment, and learn from others. Start with the basics like knife skills, sautéing, roasting, grilling, and braising. Once you feel comfortable with these techniques, move on to more advanced ones such as sous vide cooking, working with alginates, and fermentation.

Read cookbooks, watch videos, and attend workshops or classes to expand your knowledge. Don't be afraid to ask questions and learn from fellow chefs, as each one has their own unique approach and experience. Observe how different chefs work in their kitchens and take note of their techniques, methods, and tips.

Remember that learning never stops. The culinary world is vast and ever-evolving, and there is always something new to discover. Stay curious, open-minded, and passionate about your craft, and you will continue to grow and develop as a chef.

As Juno and Kris continued their in-depth conversation, the night sky outside the window bathed the room in a tranquil, dim light. It seemed as if time had paused, allowing the two chefs to explore the intricacies of the culinary world without any interruptions. The soft glow from the moon illuminated the scattered chess pieces on the board, creating a peaceful atmosphere that fostered their exchange of knowledge and wisdom. The air around them was filled with anticipation and curiosity, as Juno eagerly listened to Kris's insights, ready to take on new challenges in his culinary journey.

Juno: Explain the importance of technique then.

Kris: If we're using the analogy of paintbrushes, technique is what's going to allow you to take all the colors and turn them into images. The colors are all your ingredients and flavors, and even though everyone may have access to the same ingredients, not everyone can create beautiful art. The best chefs have a deep understanding of technique, allowing them to manipulate the ingredients and paint a beautiful picture.

Juno: Which skills and techniques do I need to know as a chef?

Kris: While all skills and techniques are important, there is a hierarchy to them. You need one to progress to the next. The beginner needs knife skills, then they move on to pan skills. In the world of knife skills, there are many things that you could learn to cut, from produce to meat and fish. Then there's a level of refinement to your knife cuts like dicing, slicing, brunoise, tourné, and so on.

Then there's the fabrication of animals like whole animal butchery, breaking down subprimals, and portioning. Next, there's learning how to transform those products through dry heat and moist heat cooking methods. Then there are techniques that are neither heat cooking nor knife work, like brining, curing, fermenting, and preserving. And of course, there's the whole world of sweets, pastries, bread, and desserts. Within all of this, there are varying degrees of complexity, finesse, and refinement.

Juno: What do you mean by finesse?

Kris: Finesse is an elegant, precise, or refined way in which you can transform and handle products. It's about how you move in the kitchen, like martial arts or dance. Think of it as having your black belt in kitchen karate. It's taking the extra steps when

49

preparing ingredients, even if it means just a slight enhancement, such as removing the skins from tomatoes to make them easier to digest. It's ensuring that every single knife cut is precise and exactly the same as the one before. It's about perfectly cooking a piece of fish in a pan or making sure a medium-rare steak is well-rested and evenly cooked from end to end when sliced. When you've mastered your techniques, the next level is to refine them through finesse.

Juno: What is more important, techniques or recipes?
Kris: Of the two, techniques are going to be superior. A recipe is a guide, but it has no soul; as the chef, it's your job to bring the recipe to life. If you learn one recipe and master it, you've gained one thing. Yet, if you master a technique, you master every variation and recipe of the technique. Take risotto, for example: if you master one recipe for mushroom risotto, then you've only gained one recipe. But if you master the risotto technique, you then master 10,000 variations of the technique.

Juno: What is more important, taste or presentation?
Kris: While they are both important, they serve different purposes. The presentation allows you to express creativity and artistic talent. Learning to balance different colors and shapes on the plate will affect how the dish is eaten. The guest first eats with their eyes, as they say, and creating a beautiful dish can be extremely satisfying for a chef.

However, ultimately taste is what will define your dish and the experience of the guest. The most beautiful dish you've ever seen may not always be the most delicious. Beautiful presentation, like art, can be a passing fad; however, the flavor will last with you and leave an imprint on your memory. Strong arguments can be made for both sides, but consider this: if you were served a dish of beautifully prepared yet rotting food or poorly presented delicious food, which one would you choose?

Juno: I see, I have never thought of it this way. When creating dishes, what is important to know?
Kris: Make sure that it fits the concept for the restaurant where you are serving it. It would make no sense to serve an Italian pasta dish in an Indian restaurant. Yet many times, as chefs, we want to express what we know and don't fully think through the impact that the dish may have on the restaurant.

Another thing is to ensure there is a story behind your dish and that everything on the plate has a purpose. Your dish should not be an exercise in vanity to showcase what you know only to impress yourself and not the guest. Lastly, make sure it is delicious. Ultimately, this will be the only thing that matters in the end. If you've designed a delicious dish yet it is not beautiful, you can always rework the presentation. However, if you design a beautiful dish that is not delicious, it is much more difficult to correct.

Juno: Can I create dishes for the sake of creativity?
Kris: Yes, absolutely, and you should. You should constantly be experimenting with new techniques, ingredients, methods, recipes, and presentations. You are going to make mistakes along the way, but this is how you learn. Evaluate where the mistakes were made and learn from them because it may not be a bad idea, just simply poorly executed. Keep refining a dish and experimenting creatively until the dish is ready to be put on the menu or presented to your chef for feedback.

Juno: Is there a strategy when designing menus?

Kris: In designing menus, there should be a balanced offering of healthy and indulgent items. A range of meats, vegetables, cooking methods, hot and cold, and sweet and savory dishes should be included. The menu should narrate the chef's story, the current time and place, the cuisine's history, and culture. The menu should be relevant to the seasons and highlight local products. The language should be guest-friendly, and items should be familiar so they can be ordered easily.

In terms of strategy, 70% of your menu should consist of items that will drive most of the restaurant's revenue, while the remaining 30% can be experimental. This balance ensures a profitable operation while still allowing space for creativity and innovation.

Chapter 7
Personal Growth and
Career Development

Personal Growth and Career Development

The time-stilled world outside seemed an appropriate backdrop for a conversation about personal growth and career development. Juno, eager to learn from Kris's vast experience, took a deep breath and prepared to ask the questions that he had been thinking about. The older chef, sensing the change in conversation, leaned back in the chair, took a sip of coffee, and smiled gently.

Juno: How can I ensure constant growth and development in my career as a chef?
Kris: This is a never-ending journey, and you will always discover things you don't know. The industry will move forward—sometimes slowly, other times at a dizzying pace. Embrace the mindset of a student. Read, watch, and most importantly, cook! Eat other people's food, sit down and discuss their cultures. In every conversation, one of you is the teacher, the other a student. Learn from those moments.

Juno paused for a moment, taking in the advice. Nodding in agreement, feeling motivated to embrace this mindset.

Juno: How do I stay up to date on what's new in the market? How can I remain relevant?

Kris: Pay attention to what's getting attention. It's important to explore new and interesting things, discovering new techniques, trends, flavors, and types of cuisine. Keep in mind that trends are short-lived, while focusing on the classics can lead to slower, more sustained growth. Find a balance between the two.

Juno: How important is networking in the culinary world, and how can I build my professional network?

Kris: A strong network will lead to multiple opportunities. Don't burn bridges with chefs—you never know when you may need to cross them again. Always be professional in your interactions, and spend time with people who inspire you to become better. Attend events, food festivals, chef gatherings, and associations. By expanding your network and maintaining good relationships, others will become advocates for you.

Juno thought about the importance of networking and vowed to make it a priority.

Juno: Should I consider furthering my education through culinary school or other programs?

Kris: Yes, but it doesn't necessarily have to be school. If you have the means, then you should. However, do not limit yourself to formal education alone. In today's world, there are many ways to educate yourself, but the most important way is to act.

Juno: If you're not always around, how can I find a mentor?

Kris: Even if I were always around, I would expect you to find more mentors. A mentor should be someone in a position you aspire to have. They should be proven, wise, generous with

55

their time, and patient. To find a mentor, simply ask. Be respectful of their time and follow through with their guidance.

Juno: What if they say no when I ask them to be my mentor?
Kris: Then ask someone else and keep asking. Every no gets you closer to a yes. Be persistent.

Juno: What's the best way for me to repay my mentor?
Kris: A good mentor will only expect you to become the best version of yourself. You living up to your potential is paying them back.

Juno started to think about how the culinary industry could become all-consuming, often resulting in chefs and cooks losing themselves and their loved ones. Wanting to achieve balance between cooking and personal time was a priority.

Juno: How can I manage work-life balance?
Kris: Establish boundaries and be transparent about them when taking a job. Be upfront with your new chef and let them know what's important to you. If you let them know that nothing is important, they will assume what's important to them is important to you.

Juno: But isn't it a chef's job to be at the restaurant all the time?
Kris: It's a chef's job to make sure the restaurant is well run. Take care of your business at work, create a great workplace culture, implement systems and processes, and build up those around you. When you've done that, this will allow you the flexibility to leave the restaurant when needed without worrying that it will fall apart in your absence. Trust that you've trained your team well.

Juno: What about when I bring the stress home from work?
Kris: It's easier said than done to leave work at work and home at home, but be fully present with your loved ones when you're home. Smile, be kind, and do the same at work.

Juno: How do I deal with high-pressure situations?
Kris: High-pressure situations are synonymous with kitchens. Eat right, hydrate, get a good night's rest, have a wellness routine, and don't forget to breathe. Pause, reflect, journal, and talk to loved ones. Most importantly, when you need a break, take one. There isn't a job out there worth sacrificing your mental health.

Juno: How do I identify my unique strengths and find my own voice?
Kris: Initially, you'll copy others and express their ideas. As you get more comfortable, you'll create on your own. Exercise your creative muscles, and the more you do, the more your creativity will grow. Then, you will stand on your own two feet.

Juno: I want to be the head chef one day. When will I be ready?
Kris: Don't be in such a rush. Enjoy your time as a sous chef, learn from your own experience and from your chef. It's better to become a good chef later than a bad one today. The more quality time you spend as a cook, sous chef, and other positions, the better prepared you'll be as a head chef.

Chapter 8
The Fight

The Fight

As they sat there, staring at each other and playing move after move on the chessboard, Juno felt like Kris was walking a razor's edge. No matter which way Juno moved a piece, Kris always had the right countermove. Not a second seemed to move on the clock, and Juno's frustration with the conversation grew.

Juno wondered if Kris could still understand what it was like to be a sous chef since it had been years since he held that position. Juno recalled times being frustrated with Kris for not being there when he needed help, and now Kris seemed to have all the answers.

Juno: This conversation can be frustrating. I feel like you're contradicting yourself. Sometimes you say work hard and have discipline, but other times you say take your time. You tell me to hold people accountable, but then you also say to be gentle and understanding. Which one is it?

Kris: Do you expect this conversation to be like a cookbook, with precise measurements guaranteeing a perfect outcome every time? Isn't it possible that there could be multiple solutions to the same problem? Perhaps your descriptions of situations are lacking key details that would affect the outcomes?

Juno: No, I've laid out the details, and sometimes you've given multiple answers to the same question.

Kris: The way you'd speak to a child isn't the same way you'd speak to a teenager or someone in their 20s, 30s, 50s, or 60s. What was difficult when you were a toddler is easy when you're an adolescent. And what was easy in your youth might be difficult in your senior years. Your mindset of what is difficult in your first week as a sous chef will be laughable after you become a head chef. So, no, not every answer can be the same. People, mindsets, and situations all affect the right move to make at any given time.

Juno: This is more of the same nonsense. Why can't you just give me a straight answer?

Kris: I can't do the work for you, nor can I learn for you. What I can do is teach you how to think. You need to learn how to consider every possibility and potential outcome, and how sometimes you need to yield and other times push forward. There will be times when you yield when you should've pushed forward and vice versa. But how will you know if you don't experience those times yourself? I can't experience them for you; I'm not you.

Juno: I can think of specific times when I was working in the kitchen and my prep list was overwhelming. I barely got it done, and you didn't help me even though you knew it was a lot of work. You just sipped your coffee and played chess by yourself. How was that setting a good example?

Kris: What you don't seem to remember is that I also had a list of work to do, but I'm efficient and completed it. You were slow and unsure of yourself, doubting your abilities and thinking you couldn't complete your list. While I played chess and sipped my coffee, I watched you. I saw you figure out ways to work more efficiently and experience the stress that came with thinking there was no way out. I saw the frustration on your face. Yet when you accomplished what you thought was unachievable, I saw the satisfaction. The next time I gave you the same list, you completed it in a shorter period. Now, when I give you the same amount, you complete it in a third of the time it took you that day. If I had done it for you, what would you have learned?

Juno: There are times when you're in the office, and I feel like I'm doing all the work.

Kris: When I'm in the office, I am working. There's a portion of my work that you don't know about or understand. I can tell you that I can do your job and my job. I understand every detail of your job, even the ones you're unaware of. Yet, I can assure you there are things I do that you haven't even considered. You look at the kitchen around you and think the food arrives on its own, the payroll gets processed magically, hiring and firing is done when no one is looking, bills get paid, and accounting is done by magical elves. The prep lists get written, the schedule gets posted, and the organization and flow of service happen by magic. Don't you ever stop and consider who does all this? How it's done? Rest assured, you would feel the chaos, maybe not immediately, but you certainly would if no one was doing any of this. A fish doesn't appreciate the water it's in until you remove it, just as we don't appreciate the air we breathe until we're underwater.

Juno: Lately, I've been coming up with all the menu ideas. I'm the creative force in the kitchen now. Yet when people come to the restaurant, they think you're making all the food, and you're taking pictures with them. I deserve the credit. When was the last time you created a dish?

Kris: I have complete authority over this restaurant, both the good and the bad. When you create a poor dish, I can't blame you in front of the customers. If the food is terrible and we lose business, I can't tell the investors it's your fault and not mine. If I have complete authority, it's for the good and the bad.

Juno: Well, then why haven't you created dishes and menu ideas lately?

Kris: Do you think I can't create menu ideas? While you've created the last five, I've created 5,000. I've forgotten more than you've learned. And while it has taken you five weeks to create five dishes, it would've taken me five minutes. The reason you're creating the dishes is to help you grow. I'm doing this for your benefit, not mine. I've had my moment to create; those muscles have been exercised already. You've barely stepped into the gym. While you resent me for having to create dishes, the only reason I've allowed you to create them is to allow you to express yourself, learn, and grow. I can remove this privilege, and you can strictly create what you're told.

Juno: I have my doubts. A few weeks back, I introduced you to a new technique that you had never heard of. I've seen the plates I've been making lately, and they're more beautiful than the ones you make. I feel like right now, I might be the stronger chef, and you're learning from me.

Kris: We were both asked to dig a 10-foot-deep hole, and I dug the first 9 1/2 feet before handing you the shovel. You then dug an extra half foot and claimed to have dug a 10-foot hole. Every technique you know in this kitchen, I taught you. You improved a completed dish that I created, but you didn't create it.

If you think you're the stronger chef, then answer these questions: How do you fix a broken hollandaise sauce? How long should you rest a piece of meat? Have you cooked 1,000 eggs without making a mistake? Have you planed and organized a banquet for 1000 people by yourself? Can you explain how to open a restaurant, close a restaurant, or negotiate with vendors? How do you course out a tasting menu without repeating an ingredient, and how do you train your staff on that tasting menu so that there are no mistakes? Can you answer any of these questions?

Juno paused for a moment, reflecting on the questions Kris had posed. Realizing that there was still so much more to learn, not only about cooking but also about managing a restaurant and leading a team. Kris had provided opportunities to grow and learn, even though it didn't always seem that way.

Juno: I understand your point. I still have a lot to learn, and I appreciate the opportunities you've given me to grow and express myself in the kitchen.
Kris: That's all I ask, Juno.

Chapter 9
The Real Test

The Real Test

As the chess game progressed, so did their conversation. This time, Juno seemed to take the lead.

Juno: There are times when I feel I might be the more skilled chef. Remember when we raced in dicing onions? I beat you.

Kris, unperturbed, nodded with a calm smile.

Kris: When I saw that you had reached a certain level of skill, I challenged you to a race. I chose a challenge that I knew you could win because I wanted you to feel victory. I'm confident in who I am, and when you beat me, it's still a win for me. My goal is to help you become a better chef than I could ever be. The true test of a great mentor is to see the person they're mentoring surpass them.

A rush of emotions surged through Juno as he began to comprehend the wisdom of Kris, who was always several steps ahead, not just in their chess games, but in real life too. The realization that the time under Kris's mentorship was nearing its end brought a wave of sadness. Kris had been Juno's guide and mentor, who had equipped them with skills and knowledge. Doubts began to creep in – was Juno really ready to step out

65

alone? Perhaps staying and continuing to learn from Kris is the better move. Yes, that's it.

Juno, raising their voice, said, "I'm not ready yet! I can't leave, I will stay here with you. I have much to learn. You've proved that over and over again throughout this conversation. I would rather be a cook under a wise chef than a sous chef under a chef I don't even know."

But Kris was adamant.

Kris: Enough! You will do no such thing. I don't want you here anymore. You must stand up on your own two feet. I have taught you everything you need to know. I have given you an example for every situation that may arise. I have taught you to think critically. I have instructed you how to play a perfect game of kitchen chess.

Juno: But I'm terrified. What if the chef is not as good as you? What if they don't mentor me?
Kris: You're only viewing the world through what it owes you. What are you going to bring to the table? Are you going to be a good sous chef? You're looking for a something-for-nothing deal. There's no such thing as a free lunch. Have you once thought that the chef may have reservations about bringing you on, that you might not be a good sous chef? You keep wanting your hand to be held, but I'm telling you, the person you need to save you is not me, it's you.

Juno: What do you mean I need to save me?
Kris: I mean that no one is going to care about you and your success more than you should. No one is going to do the work

Juno: I want to be great, but I don't know how?

Kris: If you want to be great, you could talk about it, you could read about it, and you could study greatness. But greatness cannot be achieved without action. You must act, Juno! You know all the moves, but are afraid to play the game. What separates the greats from others is their belief in themselves. Greatness comes from doing, not from overthinking. ACT!

Juno: I'm lacking the confidence.

Kris: What you're seeking is to be the exception to the rule, yet afraid to act and believe that you are the exception to the rule. Confidence comes from competence. Competence comes from experience. Experience comes from being unafraid and taking action!

Juno: Were you afraid when you had to leave your chef?

Kris: Yes, terrified. Yet every single door that opened for me required me to walk through it on my own. Remember, Juno, on the other side of fear is greatness. Be the exception to the rule.

Juno: When you are unsure and afraid who do you ask for help?

Kris: I ask Kris for help.

Juno: What do you mean? You are Kris.

Kris: If I am unwilling to help myself why should I expect someone else?

Juno: Even when it is hard?

Kris: Especially when it is hard. You can choose to be the hero of your own story or you can choose to watch someone else be the hero and save you.

Juno: And if I fail?

Kris: As long as you still have a heartbeat you get another chance. Remember you can play the game again and again. You are under no obligation to be who you were 5 minutes ago.

Now go, be great. Go and stand on your own two feet, embrace what will be difficult and face it bravely. Remember that many others have the same fears you do, but they will not act. Simply by acting, you will surpass others who are paralyzed with fear. They will have excuses to not seek greatness, but they will have to live with their decisions. I promise you Juno no other person has an advantage over you if they do not act. Action is the ultimate advantage.

Juno: Thank you, Chef. I will make you proud.

Kris: You already have, Juno.

So much had transpired in this conversation. The late-night dialogues between Juno and Kris could fill an entire library. Juno was deeply grateful for the mentorship he received from Kris. As he glanced up, the minute hand on the clock began to move again, and the restaurant started to come alive with sounds. In a moment of clarity, after thousands of games of chess, Juno recognized an opportunity. 'Checkmate,' for the first time. A smile spread across Kris's face.

About the Author

André Natera worked in professional kitchens for twenty-seven years and as an executive chef for seventeen. He currently sits on several boards and councils of culinary and food and beverage organizations, in addition to being a member of the Epicurean World Master Chef Society, inducted in 2011. He has received numerous accolades and recognition as a chef, including Best Chef, according to the Dallas Morning News in 2011 and 2012. At the beginning of 2022, Andre left running professional kitchens to focus on mentoring future chefs, including writing this book, and running the Chef's PSA

Check out the other books in the Chef's PSA Series.
How to not be the biggest idiot in the kitchen
Culinary Leadership Fundamentals
Line Cook Survival Manual
Kitchen Art of War

For more Chef's PSA content listen to the Chef's PSA podcast and follow on all our social channels @ChefsPSA.

www.chefspsa.com

Made in United States
Orlando, FL
10 September 2024

51312494R00046